THE U.S. CIVIL WAR

A Chronology of a Divided Nation

BY AMANDA PETERSON

Consultant:
Lyde Cullen Sizer, PhD
Professor of U.S. Cultural and Intellectual History
Sarah Lawrence College
Bronxville, New York

CAPSTONE PRESS
a capstone imprint

Connect is published by Capstone Press,
1710 Roe Crest Drive, North Mankato, Minnesota 56003
www.capstonepub.com

Library of Congress Cataloging-in-Publication Data
Peterson, Amanda, 1980–
  The U.S. Civil War : a chronology of a divided nation / by Amanda Peterson.
      pages cm.—(Connect. The Civil War)
  Summary: "The Civil War was a bloody 4-year battle. Follow the war from the first
shots fired on Fort Sumter to General Lee's surrender at Appomattox, and see how
America's War Between the States unfolded. Meets Common Core standards for
analyzing chronology text structures. Perfect for Common Core studies on analyzing
the chronology of an event"—Provided by publisher.
  Includes bibliographical references and index.
  ISBN 978-1-4914-2010-2 (library binding)
  ISBN 978-1-4914-2163-5 (paperback)
  ISBN 978-1-4914-2169-7 (ebook PDF)
1. United States—History—Civil War, 1861–1865—Juvenile literature. I. Title.
  E468.P49 2015
  973.702'02—dc23   2014023654

Editorial Credits
Adrian Vigliano, editor; Veronica Scott, designer; Wanda Winch, media researcher;
Kathy McColley, production specialist

Photo Credits
(The Day is Ours) by Dale Gallon, Courtesy of Gallon Historical Art, www.gallon.
com, cover; Bridgeman Images: ©Look and Learn/Private Collection, 25 (top), Gilder
Lehrman Collection, New York, USA, 29, Peter Newark American Pictures/Private
Collection, 30-31; Capstone, 8, 23 (t); Courtesy of Hal Jespersen, 39 (t); CriaImages.
com: Jay Robert Nash Collection, 7, 17 (middle), 18, 22-23, 40; Dreamstime: Bambi
L. Dingman, 34-35; Getty Images: Fotosearch, 19, Hulton Archive, 25 (bottom); The
Granger Collection, NYC, 36; iStockphoto: Duncan1890, 13 (all); Library of Congress:
Prints and Photographs Division, 5, 6, 9, 10-11, 12, 14-15 (all), 20, 21, 24, 26, 27,
28, 32-33, 34 (m), 38-39, 39 (b), 42, 43, 44-45 (all); National Archives and Records
Administration, 41; Shutterstock: Ekaterina Romanova (ornate frames), Ensuper,
cover (grunge colors), Extezy (vintage calligraphic elements), f-f-f-f (old calligraphic
décor elements), GarryKillan (damask ornamental designs), Lucy Baldwin (rust
abstract design), nikoniano (grunge stripe design), wacomka (vintage floral
background); Thinkstock: iStockphoto/Michael Poe, 37; www.historicalimagebank.
com, Painting by Don Troiani, 16-17

Printed in the United States of America in Stevens Point, Wisconsin.
092014   008479WZS15

TABLE OF CONTENTS

A NATION TORN APART 4

WAR BEGINS 10

BATTLES 20

TURNING POINT 32

THE WAR ENDS 40

GLOSSARY 46

READ MORE 47

CRITICAL THINKING USING THE COMMON CORE . . . 47

INTERNET SITES 48

INDEX 48

A NATION TORN APART

NEIGHBOR VERSUS NEIGHBOR

In 1861 the U.S. Civil War (1861–1865) began. Northern states made up the Union. Southern states that **seceded** from the Union formed the Confederacy. The war lasted four years and took the lives of more than 620,000 people.

The war was fought over two big issues: states' rights and slavery. Southerners wanted their own country. They thought state governments should have more control over what happened inside their borders. This included the right to decide if slavery would be allowed. Many Northerners did not support the Southern states leaving the United States. They supported President Lincoln and argued the Constitution prevented states from leaving the Union.

As the Civil War continued its focus shifted to **abolishing** slavery. The Northern states had begun abolishing slavery before the war. Many white Northerners still held racist ideas, but they also thought slavery was wrong. The Confederacy continued to allow slavery. More than 30 percent of Confederate households owned slaves. **Plantation** owners believed they would not make money without slavery. They were also worried that the Northerners would not allow slavery to happen in new states.

secede—to formally withdraw from a group or an organization, often to form another organization
abolish—to put an end to something officially
plantation—a large farm found in warm areas

TIMELINE OF THE SLAVERY DEBATE

The first black slaves arrived in what would become the state of Virginia in 1619. The issue of slavery was debated from that day forward. Here are some other important events that led to the United States' Civil War.

Many slaves worked in plantation fields, growing crops for food or materials such as cotton.

1789
The Constitution of the United States is adopted. It mentions slavery in a few places, but does not end the practice.

1793
Eli Whitney invents the cotton gin. Southern plantations continue to rely on slavery to keep up with cotton production.

1820
The Missouri Compromise keeps a delicate balance between slave and free states.

1831
Nat Turner leads a deadly slave rebellion in Southampton County, Virginia.

1850
The Compromise of 1850 admits California as a free state and organized Utah and New Mexico territories.

1852
Harriet Beecher Stowe's best-selling book *Uncle Tom's Cabin* is published.

1854
The Kansas-Nebraska Act creates Kansas and Nebraska territories while effectively repealing the Missouri Compromise.

1857
The Supreme Court rules in the case of *Dred Scott v. Sanford* that blacks can never become citizens of the United States.

1859
Radical abolitionist John Brown leads a group in seizing Harpers Ferry in West Virginia. His plan to start a slave rebellion fails and he is hanged.

PRESIDENTIAL ELECTION OF 1860

When Abraham Lincoln won the presidential election of 1860, many Southerners were angry. They did not trust Lincoln and feared he would end slavery. Lincoln's election caused Southerners to do what Northern politicians feared most. They started taking steps to secede from the Union.

Fact

Lincoln was so disliked by Southerners that many polling places did not even list his name on ballots.

Abraham Lincoln
1809–1865

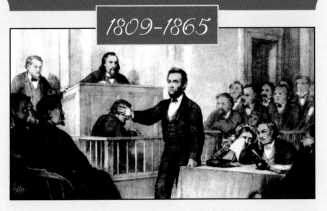

Born in 1809 in Kentucky, Abraham Lincoln had many jobs before becoming a lawyer. In 1858 he ran for the U.S. Senate against Stephen Douglas. During his **campaign** Lincoln described the United States as a 'house divided': "I believe this government cannot endure permanently half slave and half free. I do not expect the Union to be dissolved. I do not expect the house to fall; but I do expect it will cease to be divided. It will become all one thing or all the other." Lincoln lost the Senate race, but won the presidential election of 1860. As president Lincoln was popular with some Northerners. He was re-elected in 1864. Although he lived to see the fall of the Confederate States of America, his life was cut short. Lincoln was **assassinated**. He was shot by a Southern sympathizer on April 14, 1865, and died the next morning.

campaign—organized actions and events with a specific goal, such as being elected
assassinate—to murder a person who is well-known or important

A New Nation

South Carolina was the first state to leave the Union, officially seceding on December 20, 1860. All 169 state legislators voted for secession.

Soon Mississippi, Florida, Alabama, Georgia, Louisiana, and Texas also seceded. In February of 1861, these states called themselves a new country—the Confederate States of America. Representatives of the first six states to secede elected Jefferson Davis as president. By May, Virginia, Arkansas, Tennessee, and North Carolina had joined the Confederate States of America as well.

Eastern states during the Civil War

Union state (North)

Border state

Upper South—Confederate state seceding after Fort Sumter, 1861

Lower South—Confederate state seceding before Fort Sumter, 1861

Capital city

CANADA

Maine

Vt. N.H.

New York

Mass.

Conn.

R.I.

Iowa

Mich.

Pennsylvania

Gettysburg

Antietam

New Jersey

Illinois

Indiana

Ohio

Md.

Delaware

Bull Run

Washington, D.C.

Chancellorsville

Fredericksburg

Missouri

W. Va.

Richmond

Kentucky

Va.

Petersburg

Appomattox

Fort Donelson

Fort Henry

Tennessee

North Carolina

Bentonville

Shiloh

Arkansas

Memphis

Chattanooga

Atlanta

South Carolina

Miss.

Alabama

Atlantic Ocean

Vicksburg

Georgia

Fort Sumter

Savannah

Louisiana

New Orleans

Gulf of Mexico

Florida

0   300 miles

0   300 kilometers

N

W   E

S

Jefferson Davis

1808-1889

Born in 1808 in Kentucky, Jefferson Davis studied at the United States' military academy, West Point. Davis served in the military and owned a plantation in Mississippi. He served in both the U.S. House of Representatives and the U.S. Senate. Davis believed that the South's **economy** needed slavery. He supported the rights of Southern states. Davis took office as provisional president of the Confederate States of America on February 18, 1861. In November Confederate voters elected him president. As the Civil War drew to an end, Davis was forced to flee the South's capital city of Richmond, Virginia. He was captured by Union troops on May 10, 1865. He spent two years in prison awaiting trial, but he was never tried. His case eventually was dropped. Davis continued to defend the Southern cause until his death in 1889.

economy—the ways in which a country handles its money and resources

WAR BEGINS

LINCOLN TAKES OFFICE

Lincoln took office on March 4, 1861. He did not think slavery should be allowed in new states. Lincoln also believed the Constitution made it illegal for states to leave the Union. Lincoln said war would only happen if started by Southerners. He hoped the Confederate states would rejoin the Union peacefully.

Confederate leaders did not want to rejoin the Union. President Davis sent **delegates** to Washington. Lincoln would not meet or negotiate with them—to do so might be considered an official recognition of the Confederacy. Instead, the two sides communicated through messengers.

The delegates wanted the Confederacy to control Union forts located in Southern states. One important fort was the Union's Fort Sumter in South Carolina. The soldiers protecting the fort were running out of food and supplies. Lincoln had to decide if Fort Sumter should be given to a country he did not think really existed. His other option was to keep the fort under Union control and send supplies.

On April 8, 1861, Confederates learned the Union was sending boats filled with supplies to Fort Sumter. Confederates responded by demanding that the Union immediately surrender the fort. The Union refused.

Union Major Robert Anderson moved his soldiers into Fort Sumter after South Carolina seceded. He hoped the fort would protect them.

delegate—someone who represents other people at a meeting

THE FIRST SHOT

Hopes for peace were destroyed on April 12, 1861. That morning Confederate troops fired on Fort Sumter. The Union had few supplies and soldiers. The two sides fought for about 33 hours before the fort surrendered. No troops had been killed in the battle. On April 14 a South Carolina military unit raised the Confederacy's Stars and Bars flag at Fort Sumter. The Civil War had begun.

Union troops in Fort Sumter did not return fire for the first two hours of battle because they did not have enough ammunition.

Flags of War

The United States' 33-Star Flag

When the war started, the United States' flag had 13 stripes and 33 stars. There was one star for each state in the Union. Lincoln decided to keep all the stars on the flag during the war. He was fighting to save the Union. No stars could be removed.

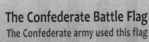

The Stars and Bars

The first flag of the Confederacy was nicknamed the "Stars and Bars." The flag had three stripes and seven stars. The stars were symbols of the first seven states to join the Confederacy. The flag created confusion because it was too similar to the Union flag.

The Stainless Banner

The Confederacy needed a new flag. This flag added six stars. Four stars were for the states that seceded after Fort Sumter. The last two stars stood for the states of Kentucky and Missouri. Those states had not seceded. The Confederate states still considered them part of the South. This flag also caused problems. There was too much white. It looked like a surrender flag.

The Third National Confederate Flag

A red stripe was added to the edge of the flag to make it look less like a surrender flag. This change was made just before the war ended.

The Confederate Battle Flag

The Confederate army used this flag during battle. Army units mostly used a square version of the flag.

RALLY THE TROOPS

Lincoln and Davis worked to build their armies. The Union's army had about 16,000 soldiers. The majority of them were in the western part of the country. Lincoln first asked for 75,000 volunteer soldiers from Union states. Lincoln asked the first batch of Union volunteers to agree to three months of service.

Davis had to build the Confederate army and navy from nothing. Many people did not think the Civil War would last very long.

Men of all ages volunteered to fight, though most were younger than 30. Soldiers were supposed to be at least 18 years old, but this was often ignored. Up to 20 percent were under 18. Boys as young as 12 served as buglers and drummers. Most of the volunteers had never fought in a battle. They needed a lot of training.

Union officers knew they needed a lot of time to build a strong army. But the politicians wanted a quick war. Lincoln agreed that the Union army was inexperienced, but he believed the Confederate soldiers were also unprepared. He ordered the Union's army into battle.

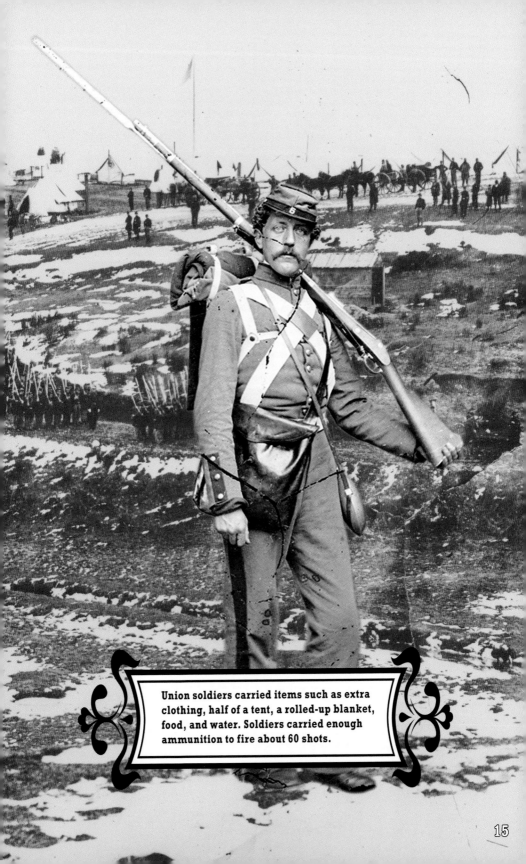

Union soldiers carried items such as extra clothing, half of a tent, a rolled-up blanket, food, and water. Soldiers carried enough ammunition to fire about 60 shots.

Fact

The Union and Confederacy often gave the same battle different names. The Union often used names of physical features or landmarks to name battles. The Confederates mostly used the names of nearby places. For example, Confederates knew the Union's First Battle of Bull Run as First Manassas.

First Battle of Bull Run (First Manassas)

On July 16, the Union army marched toward Manassas Junction in Virginia. They met the Confederate army on July 21 at a creek called Bull Run. A long day of fighting began.

Soldiers on both sides grew tired. Confederate General Barnard Elliott Bee saw Confederate General Thomas Jackson pushing his men to keep fighting. General Bee thought Jackson stood strong like a "stone wall" under enemy fire. "Stonewall" Jackson would become a hero of the Confederate army.

Reinforcements helped the Confederates beat the Union. The Union was forced to retreat. The Confederates did not pursue the Union soldiers. Instead, they celebrated. Many thought they had not only won the battle, but also the war. But the war was only beginning.

General Bee

H.G.

WATCHING THE WAR

Civilians watched the First Battle of Bull Run from a few miles away. They had traveled from Washington, D.C., to see the fighting. Some picnicked while watching the battle. A few of the civilians moved closer to a spot near a field hospital. Retreating Union soldiers moved through the civilians' location. The spectators were swept up into the group and fled with the soldiers back to Washington, D.C.

Politicians including congressmen and Rhode Island governor William Sprague joined the spectators at Bull Run. Most observers expected an easy Union victory.

Civil War Nurses

The Civil War was a medical nightmare. Neither side was prepared for the high number of wounded soldiers. At first most nurses were male. Many people didn't like women working as nurses because it was not "ladylike." However, large numbers of women on both sides volunteered to serve as nurses. Their work supported soldiers in many ways. Nurses helped with **amputations,** dressed wounds, and gave out medicine. They reduced the spread of disease by cleaning hospitals and medical equipment. More than 20,000 women worked as Union nurses.

amputate—to cut off someone's arm, leg, or other body part, usually because the part is damaged

After the loss at Bull Run, Union generals worked to improve their soldiers' training. But Lincoln was unhappy with General George McClellan. Lincoln thought McClellan was too cautious. He wanted McClellan's soldiers to capture the Confederate capital city of Richmond, Virginia, but McClellan was slow to act.

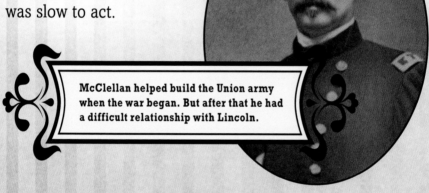

McClellan helped build the Union army when the war began. But after that he had a difficult relationship with Lincoln.

THE WESTERN FRONT

General Ulysses S. Grant led part of the Union army in the western states and **frontier**. Grant was less cautious than McClellan. "Find out where your enemy is," Grant said. "Get at him as soon as you can. Strike at him as hard as you can and as often as you can, and keep moving on." Grant became known for refusing to accept an enemy's surrender unless it was immediate and without conditions.

Ulysses S. Grant

1822–1885

Ulysses S. Grant served in the army until leaving in 1854. When the Civil War started, he rejoined the army. He commanded a group of volunteers. Grant was a great leader. Lincoln once said of him, "I can't spare this man, he fights." In 1864 Lincoln put Grant in charge of the Union army. When the war ended, Grant was kind to the surrendering Confederates. He allowed officers to return home with some weapons and other supplies. Grant was elected president in 1868 and served two terms. He died in 1885.

Fact

Battles took place across the Union, Confederacy, and western frontier. Historians estimate that fighting took place in 10,000 locations.

frontier—the far edge of a settled area, where few people live

The Battle of Shiloh (Battle of Pittsburg Landing)

Lincoln was impressed by Grant's victories. Grant was not afraid to defend the Union by bringing men into battle. As Grant's soldiers won battles, they followed retreating Confederates further south. But the Confederates wanted the Union army to follow them. Grant thought the armies would meet in Mississippi. He allowed his soldiers to rest. They waited for reinforcements. Grant and his men were not prepared for what would happen.

On April 6, 1862, Confederate General Albert Johnston's soldiers surprised Grant's troops. The two-day-battle that followed became known as the Battle of Shiloh (Battle of Pittsburg Landing). The first day was intense and chaotic. Soldiers were unprepared. That evening 25,000 Union reinforcements arrived. On the second day, the Union outnumbered the Confederates. By afternoon the Confederates were forced to retreat. The Union won, but both sides paid a large price. More than 23,000 soldiers were killed, wounded, captured, or missing.

Key Battles of the Civil War

Grant's troops were almost driven to retreat on the first day of Shiloh. But on the second day they fought back and finally won the battle.

WOMEN AT WAR

During the war, women began working the jobs men had left to become soldiers. Women managed plantations and farms, ran stores, nursed soldiers, and worked in factories. They provided food, crops, clothing, ammunition, and other items.

Women also organized more than 20,000 aid societies. These groups raised money and collected items and food for soldiers. In the North many of these groups were part of the United States Sanitary Commission. This organization helped set up battlefield hospitals and transported soldiers to receive care.

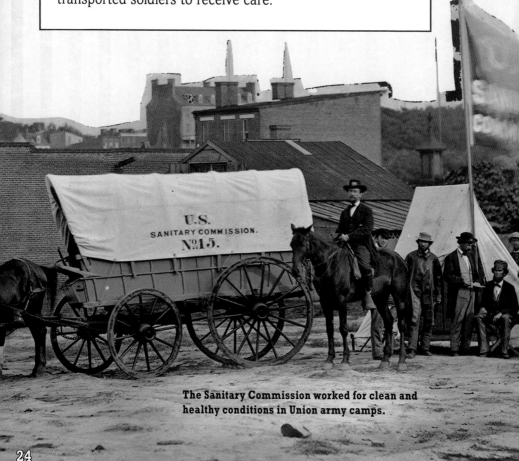

The Sanitary Commission worked for clean and healthy conditions in Union army camps.

Women on both sides became spies. White women could sometimes cross into enemy territory without being searched. They carried important information, weapons, and medicines to troops.

Harriet Tubman

1820-1913

Harriet Tubman was born into slavery around 1820 in Maryland. In 1849 she ran away and found freedom in Pennsylvania. In the 1850s she joined the Underground Railroad. This network of safe places helped bring slaves north so they could be free. Helping slaves escape was a dangerous job. Tubman was one of the Railroad's "conductors." She safely brought around 300 slaves to freedom. During the Civil War Tubman played an important role in supporting the Union. She worked as a nurse and spied on Confederates. She remained a strong supporter of equality for blacks and women until her death in 1913.

Lincoln Wants More

McClellan finally did as Lincoln wished and directed his soldiers toward Richmond. McClellan's men met Confederate General Robert E. Lee's troops in the Battle of Oak Grove (Battle of French's Field) on June 25, 1862. Lee's men were well prepared. McClellan's soldiers withdrew from fighting that evening. This move gave Lee time to prepare for the next battle.

Robert E. Lee

1807–1870

Robert E. Lee was a great leader and military **strategist.** Lincoln asked him to lead the Union army, but Lee refused. He was loyal to his home state of Virginia. Lee became a Confederate general and led soldiers in battle until the end of the war. After surrendering to Grant on April 9, 1865, Lee told his men: "I have done the best I could for you. My heart is too full to say more."

Oak Grove marked the first of a series of battles that took place over one week. During the Seven Days' battles more than 30,000 soldiers were killed, wounded, or missing. The Union only had one defeat in the battles. But McClellan still chose to have his men retreat.

The two armies met again in Maryland on September 17, 1862. The Battle of Antietam (Battle of Sharpsburg) was the war's bloodiest day. More than 23,100 soldiers were killed, wounded, or missing. The Confederates retreated. Lincoln had sent a message asking McClellan to "Destroy the rebel army, if possible." But six weeks passed before McClellan began to follow the Confederates. Lincoln had had enough. He removed McClellan from his position.

The Battle of Antietam did not have a clear winner, but Lincoln claimed it was a victory for the Union.

strategist—someone who is good at making plans to accomplish a goal

EMANCIPATION PROCLAMATION

On September 22, 1862, Lincoln issued a preliminary version of the Emancipation Proclamation. It said that Lincoln planned to free all slaves in Confederate states by January 1, 1863. This would happen if rebel states did not surrender to the Union before that date.

Lincoln believed that in order to win the war, he had to free the slaves. This would allow blacks to join the Union army. It would also hurt the South's economy by leaving fewer workers on plantations. Finally, the Emancipation Proclamation gave the Union a strong focus of fighting to end slavery. On January 1, 1863, the final Emancipation Proclamation declared slaves in Confederate states free. But Southerners refused to follow Lincoln's orders.

Lincoln read the Emancipation Proclamation to his cabinet before delivering it publicly.

All SLAVES were made FREEMEN
BY ABRAHAM LINCOLN,
PRESIDENT OF THE UNITED STATES,
JANUARY 1st, 1863.
Come, then, able-bodied COLORED MEN, to the nearest United States Camp, and fight for the
STARS AND STRIPES.

A paper from 1863 asked black men to join the Union army. The Emancipation Proclamation made this type of recruitment possible.

Contraband Camps

During the Civil War about half a million slaves escaped. Slaves who sought Union army protection were placed in special areas called contraband camps. The camps were often dirty and full of disease. Many Union soldiers were racist and treated escaped slaves poorly. But the camps did provide food, clothing, shelter, education, and basic health care. Escaped slaves also started their own schools and churches. Strong black communities grew out of contraband camps. By the end of the Civil War, there were more than 100 contraband camps.

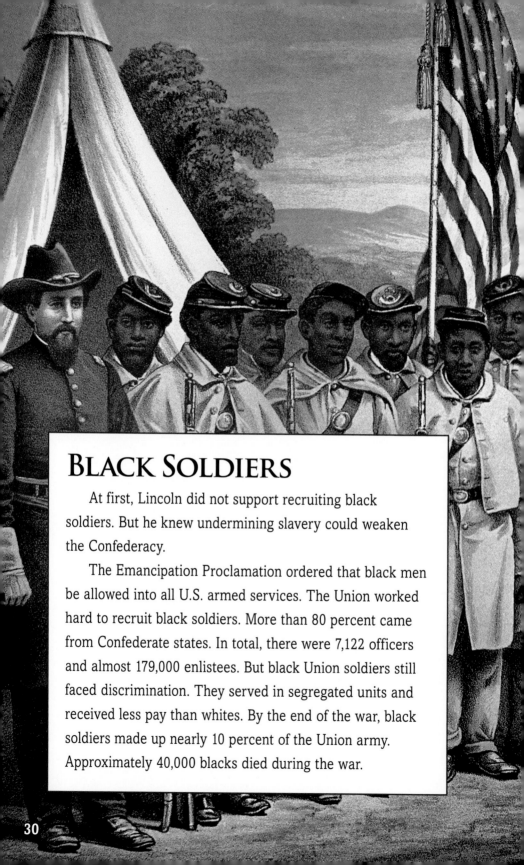

BLACK SOLDIERS

At first, Lincoln did not support recruiting black soldiers. But he knew undermining slavery could weaken the Confederacy.

The Emancipation Proclamation ordered that black men be allowed into all U.S. armed services. The Union worked hard to recruit black soldiers. More than 80 percent came from Confederate states. In total, there were 7,122 officers and almost 179,000 enlistees. But black Union soldiers still faced discrimination. They served in segregated units and received less pay than whites. By the end of the war, black soldiers made up nearly 10 percent of the Union army. Approximately 40,000 blacks died during the war.

Blacks also served for the Confederacy, though many did so unwillingly. The Confederates recruited blacks to fill positions left vacant by whites serving on the battlefields. But the Confederate government would not enlist blacks as soldiers. In the final months of the war, General Lee desperately needed reinforcements. On March 23, 1865, blacks were allowed to serve in the Confederate army in non-combat positions.

A recruitment poster for the Union army showed a group of black soldiers at Camp William Penn near Philadelphia.

TURNING POINT

As the war dragged on, Lincoln was frustrated. He could not understand how the Union was losing battles. The North had far more resources and supplies than the Confederacy. It did not make sense that the Confederates could force his men to retreat.

Lee thought the Union army was weak. He wanted to bring his troops into the North to win a major battle. If he could beat the Union army on its own soil, he thought Lincoln might end the war.

On July 1, 1863, Confederate and Union troops met at Gettysburg, Pennsylvania. The Union was ready to fight. But Lee was not prepared. Union troops held their ground. Lee's ranks suffered greatly. After three days of battle, the Confederates retreated. More soldiers died at Gettysburg than in any other battle. The Confederate army losses were about 28,000 soldiers. The Union lost about 23,000.

Gettysburg was a turning point in the Civil War. The Union had won a major victory. The Confederacy suffered a great loss. Their supplies and men were hard to replace.

Some historians think Lee's great victory at Chancellorsville in May of 1863 caused him to believe his army could not be beaten.

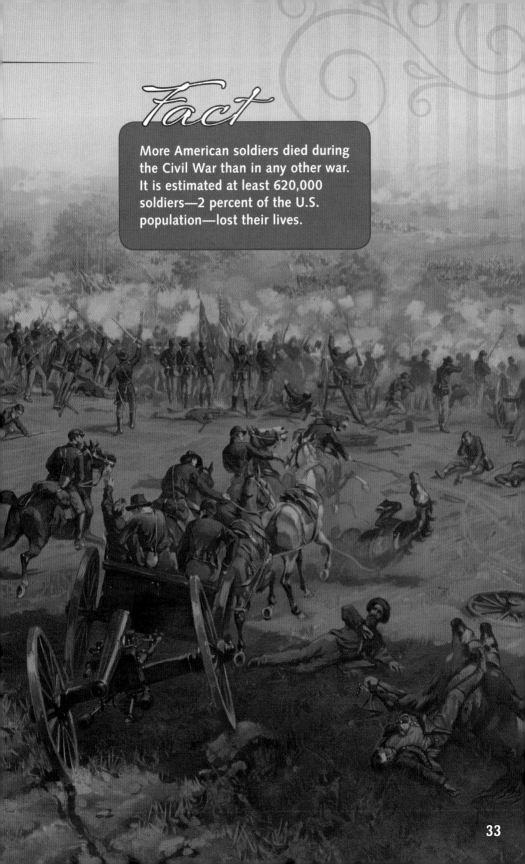

Fact

More American soldiers died during the Civil War than in any other war. It is estimated at least 620,000 soldiers—2 percent of the U.S. population—lost their lives.

GETTYSBURG ADDRESS

Lincoln gave his Gettysburg Address on November 19, 1863. It was part of the dedication ceremony for the Soldiers' National Cemetery. His speech was short and powerful. Lincoln honored the soldiers who died at Gettysburg. He wanted to use the soldiers' courageous acts to inspire the Union to keep fighting. Lincoln spoke these powerful words: "from these honored dead we take increased devotion to that cause for which they gave the last full measure of devotion—that we here highly resolve that these dead shall not have died in vain, that this nation under God shall have a new birth of freedom, and that government of the people, by the people, for the people shall not perish from the earth."

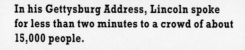

In his Gettysburg Address, Lincoln spoke for less than two minutes to a crowd of about 15,000 people.

3RD N.Y.
DEPENDENT BATTERY
ARTILLERY BRIGADE
SIXTH CORPS

JULY 2 & 3, 1863

Fact

The Soldiers' National Cemetery is now known as Gettysburg Military Park. It is the location of the graves of more than 3,500 Union soldiers who died in the Battle of Gettysburg. The cemetery holds the remains of only a few Confederate soldiers. The majority of Confederate soldiers who died at Gettysburg were moved to Southern states.

GRANT TAKES CHARGE

Grant continued to win important battles on the western front. The Siege of Vicksburg, Mississippi, began on May 18, 1863. For 47 days the Union army surrounded the city. The 29,500 Confederate troops protecting the city faced 70,000 Union soldiers. Gunfire, artillery shells, and explosives damaged the city. It became difficult for Confederate soldiers and residents to find food. They began to get sick and starve. On July 4 Confederate General Pemberton surrendered. Next Grant took control of nearby Port Hudson. The Union now controlled the Mississippi River.

On October 16 Lincoln made Grant Lieutenant General of the Union army. Grant shifted his focus to the eastern front. He wanted to take Richmond. He asked General William T. Sherman to take control of the South.

During the Siege of Vicksburg, people dug caves into the hills to find safety from the fighting.

Grant's success at Vicksburg and Port Hudson were important for the Union. His victories hurt the Confederacy by splitting it into two parts.

The Home Fronts

In the Confederacy high prices made items such as rice, corn, sugar, flour, meat, and fabric difficult to afford. Southern people faced starvation and poverty. Women began rioting. They took food, supplies, and money, and shared with those in need.

The Union passed a **draft** law to find more soldiers. Wealthy men could pay to escape the draft, but most men had no option but to enlist. Angry citizens protested. People rioted, breaking into government buildings, attacking government workers, and destroying draft records.

draft—to select men to serve in the military

THE UNION ARMY GAINS GROUND

Grant's men faced difficult battles in their attempt to take Richmond. At the same time Sherman's soldiers stormed across the South. His men destroyed many things in their path—houses, businesses, railroad tracks, and plantations. Sherman's attack on Atlanta, Georgia, started in May and ended on September 2, 1864. When the Confederates left the city, Sherman wrote to Lincoln and declared victory: "Atlanta is ours, and fairly won."

On November 8, 1864, Lincoln was reelected to a second term. One week later Sherman's men destroyed much of Atlanta. Their goal was to destroy anything the Confederates could use after the Union left. This was the beginning of Sherman's "March to the Sea." On their way to the Atlantic Ocean, Sherman's men continued to destroy buildings and resources. They captured Savannah on December 21, 1864.

Union troops pushed into South Carolina. On February 18 they took the city of Charleston. Soon, the stars and stripes were flying again over Fort Sumter.

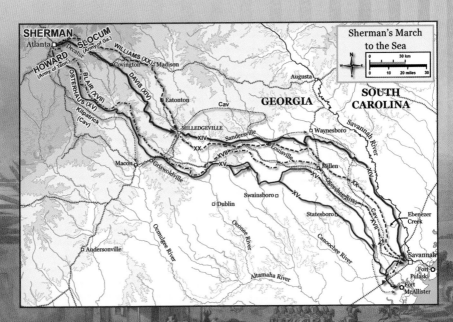

Sherman's March
to the Sea

SHERMAN
Atlanta
SLOCUM
(Army of Ga.)
Decatur
HOWARD
(Army of Tenn.)
Covington
WILLIAMS (XX)
Madison
DAVIS (XIV)
OSTERHAUS (XV)
BLAIR (XVII)
Kilpatrick
(Cav)
Eatonton
Augusta
GEORGIA
SOUTH
CAROLINA
Cav
MILLEDGEVILLE
XIV
Sandersville
Waynesboro
Savannah River
XX
XVII
Louisville
Macon
Griswoldville
XV
Millen
Oconee River
XV
Ogeechee River
Cav
XVII
Swainsboro
XV
Statesboro
Dublin
Ebenezer
Creek
Andersonville
Oconee River
Canoochee River
Savannah
Fort
Pulaski
Altamaha River
Fort
McAllister

Fact

General Sherman was a highly respected leader. After capturing Atlanta Sherman moved his soldiers across the state of Georgia. They left behind them a trail of destruction as wide as 60 miles (97 kilometers).

THE WAR ENDS

The Union continued to take control of Confederate cities. Lincoln was sworn into office for his second term on March 4, 1865. At his **inauguration** he called for "malice toward none; with charity for all." Lincoln wanted to "bind up the nation's wounds."

LEE SURRENDERS

On April 3, 1865, the Union captured Richmond. General Lee knew he had been defeated. He said, "There is nothing left for me to do but to go see General Grant, and I would rather die a thousand deaths."

On April 9, 1865, Lee and Grant met at Appomattox Court House, Virginia, to surrender. The terms of surrender allowed officers to keep their personal belongings, including some weapons. Confederates who owned a horse or mule were allowed to take them. This would help them farm when they returned to their homes.

Lee (right) was briefly held as a prisoner of war after his surrender.

inauguration—formal ceremony to swear a person into political office

When Lee returned to Richmond, he was given a hero's welcome. Many people were upset the Confederacy had lost the war, but Southerners still respected Lee. He encouraged Southerners to put the war behind them and work for unity.

The Thirteenth Amendment

The Thirteenth Amendment abolished slavery in the United States. It took effect on December 6, 1865. It is considered one of the Reconstruction amendments. One of these amendments gave freed slaves citizenship. Another provided black men with the right to vote.

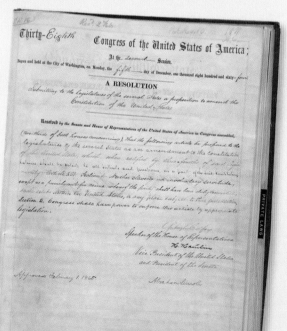

DAVIS FLEES

The Confederacy's former president, Jefferson Davis, fled Richmond on April 2, 1865. He moved through the southeastern states to avoid capture. Davis knew his army had been defeated, but he still tried to run the Confederacy. On May 10, 1865, he was arrested and imprisoned for two years.

After his imprisonment, Davis wrote a history of the Confederacy and retired in Mississippi. He died in 1889.

Fact

Fighting continued after Lee's surrender. The last battle was in Texas on May 13, 1865. It was a Confederate victory.

Lincoln's Assassination

On April 14, 1865, five days after Lee surrendered, a Southern sympathizer named John Wilkes Booth assassinated Lincoln. Booth did not agree with Lincoln's push for equality between black and white citizens. He thought that killing Lincoln might save the Confederacy. Booth shot Lincoln while he watched a play at Ford's Theatre in Washington, D.C. Lincoln died the next morning.

Lincoln's death marked the beginning of Reconstruction, another difficult period of American history. The South's economy had been destroyed. About 4 million former slaves needed support from the government. The United States had to be rebuilt.

The First Modern War

The Civil War is considered the first modern war. Both sides used new technology and inventions. This changed the way future wars were fought.

The Union and Confederate armies relied on trains to quickly move people and supplies to battles. Railroads made it possible for thousands of men to fight in a single battle.

Both sides used gas-filled balloons. Men could float above the land to spy on the enemy. They could see how many troops were coming and spy on enemy supply lines. The Union army was especially good at using balloons.

Many soldiers had powerful rifles and muskets that could hit targets hundreds of yards away. Guns became easier to load than ever before. They could also fire more bullets before needing to be reloaded.

The Civil War also changed naval warfare. Both navies used metal-covered ships called ironclads. Union and Confederate ironclads fought in the Battle of Hampton Roads in Virginia on March 9, 1862. This was the first time ironclad ships fought against one another in battle.

Thaddeus Lowe, "Chief Aeronaut" of the Union army, designed special tough balloons for military use.

The USS *Essex* was one of the most powerful river ironclads of the Civil War. The *Essex* attacked and damaged the Confederate ironclad *Arkansas* at the Siege of Vicksburg.

GLOSSARY

abolish (uh-BOL-ish)—to put an end to something officially

amputate (AM-pyuh-tayt)—to cut off someone's arm, leg, or other body part, usually because the part is damaged

assassinate (us-SASS-uh-nate)—to murder a person who is well-known or important

campaign (kam-PAYN)—organized actions and events with a specific goal, such as being elected

delegate (DEL-uh-guht)—someone who represents other people at a meeting

draft (DRAFT)—to select men to serve in the military

economy (i-KAH-nuh-mee)—the ways in which a country handles its money and resources

frontier (fruhn-TIHR)—the far edge of a settled area, where few people live

inauguration (in-aw-gyuh-RAY-shuhn)—formal ceremony to swear a person into political office

plantation (plan-TAY-shuhn)—a large farm found in warm areas; before the Civil War, plantations in the South used slave labor

reinforcements (ree-in-FORSS-muhnts)—extra troops sent into battle

secede (si-SEED)—to formally withdraw from a group or an organization, often to form another organization

strategist (STRAT-uh-jist)—someone who is good at making plans to accomplish a goal

READ MORE

Fitzgerald, Stephanie. *A Civil War Timeline.* War Timelines. North Mankato, Minn.: Capstone Press, 2014.

Nemeth, Jason D. *Voices of the Civil War: Stories from the Battlefields.* Voices Of War. Mankato, Minn.: Capstone Press, 2011.

Olson, Kay Melchisedech. *The Terrible, Awful Civil War: The Disgusting Details About Life During America's Bloodiest War.* Disgusting History. Mankato, Minn.: Capstone Press, 2010.

Rees, Bob. *The Civil War.* Living Through... Chicago: Heinemann Library, 2012.

Stanchak, John E. *Civil War.* New York: DK Pub., 2011.

CRITICAL THINKING USING THE COMMON CORE

1. The first slaves arrived in the United States in 1619. Why did it take such a long time for slavery to become illegal? (Key Ideas and Details)

2. The Confederacy had far fewer resources than the Union. What do you think allowed the Confederate army to win so many battles? (Integration of Knowledge and Ideas)

3. Which Civil War event do you think had the biggest impact on the war's outcome? Why? Use information from the book and other sources to support your answers. (Key Ideas and Details)

INTERNET SITES

FactHound offers a safe, fun way to find Internet sites related to this book. All of the sites on FactHound have been researched by our staff.

Here's all you do:

Visit *www.facthound.com*

Type in this code: 9781491420102

INDEX

battles
    Antietam (Sharpsburg), 27
    First Battle of Bull Run
    (First Manassas), 16, 17,
       18, 20
    Fort Sumter, 11, 12, 13, 38
    Gettysburg, 32, 34, 35
    Hampton Roads, 44
    Oak Grove (French's Field),
    26, 27
    Seven Days' battles, 27
    Shiloh (Pittsburg Landing),
    22, 23
    Siege of Vicksburg, 36,
    37, 45
Booth, John Wilkes, 43

Davis, Jefferson, 8, 9, 10, 14, 42
Douglas, Stephen, 7

Emancipation Proclamation,
    28, 29, 30

Gettysburg Address, 34
Grant, Ulysses S., 20, 21, 22,
    23, 36, 37, 38, 40

Lee, Robert E., 26, 31, 32, 40,
    41, 42, 43
Lincoln, Abraham, 4, 6, 7, 10,
    11, 13, 14, 20, 21, 22, 26, 27,
    28, 30, 32, 34, 36, 38, 40, 43

McClellan, George, 20, 26, 27

nurses, 19, 24, 25

Sherman, William T., 36, 38, 39
spies, 25, 44
Stowe, Harriet Beecher, 5

Tubman, Harriet, 25

United States Sanitary
    Commission, 24